A TREE WHOSE NAME I DON'T KNOW

BY GOLAN HAJI

TRANSLATED BY STEPHEN WATTS & GOLAN HAJI

A MIDSUMMER NIGHT'S PRESS

New York

Published with the support of Shubbak: A Window on Contemporary Arab Culture in a partnership with the British Council.

Acknowledgments

We want to thank all the editors and publishers where some of these translations previously appeared: *The Critical Muslim, Jadaliyya, Modern Poetry In Translation, The Wolf* & *Words Without Borders*.

The excerpt from 'A Soldier In A Madhouse' was published in *The Hundred Years' War : Modern War Poems*, edited by Neil Astley (Bloodaxe Books, 2014).

The sequence 'A Light In Water' was commissioned by Sasha Dugdale for *Modern Poetry In Translation* & appeared in its 'Great Flight' issue : No.1 2016.

'Mr. Nobody Listening To His Own Story At The Court Of King Alcinous' was commissioned by Julian May for the BBC as part of 'The Odyssey Project : My Name Is Nobody' and selections from it were broadcast on Radio 4 in April 2017.

"Box of Pain" was first published in Arabic and Danish in a limited edition artbook, published by Korridor33 (København) in 2011 together with poems by the Danish poet Kristina Stoltz.

Eight new poems were translated, commissioned by Shubbak, and were first published by *Modern Poetry In Translation* in its "A Blossom Shroud" issue, summer 2017.

New poems and translations were created with the support of Shubbak: A Window on Contemporary Arab Culture in a partnership with the British Council.

A Midsummer Night's Press
3 Norden Drive
Glen Head NY 11545
amidsummernightspress@gmail.com
www.amidsummernightspress.com

Designed by Nieves Guerra.
First edition.

ISBN-13:978-1-938334-27-6

CONTENTS

TRANSLATOR'S NOTE

I met Golan Haji at the Al-Sendian (Al-Mallajeh) Festival in Syria in 2010, a beautiful gathering of poets, artists, photographers, children, and villagers, and the last of its kind before the appalling years of rupture exploded in 2011. We've translated these poems across the intervening years whenever there was an opportunity to snatch time to sit, or walk, together—this shared space being vital because it gives the scope to directly test and coax the fluency, physicality, verve and edge of the poetry into something not too dissimilar in English. When it works (and intuitively we feel it often does) then 'a happy journey' is perhaps the most appropriate description of this dialogue of translation, and one that may afford a more life-giving take on the meaning of migration.

—Stephen Watts

from "MARCH LIGHT"

Raise your eyes
to the cloud above your head:
it's like the belly of an animal
you'd like to play with.
Snow in the shadow
covers a stone & a crumb of bread.

Do you hear the wind
between the blossoming peach branches?
Ah, you understand me?

It's morning, the air is sharper than our eyes
and no one leaves any trace
in the mirror.

* * *

I hide my hell inside me while I smile: that's my act as an actor, always & even when alone.

If I really killed everything I would be alone & dead: when I was being inattentive I did indeed kill everything & then I killed myself. And now I hate what I secretly remember & I yearn for what terrifies me. Back then I was fond of the last sip of life in a dying mouth & I was saying: my terror inhales the same air as your laughter; but I myself wasn't the one who stumbled over your shadows, to pounce on myself like a rabid dog.

What I know of the guillotine is just its name, whenever I heard it I saw the beautiful head of Marie Antoinette & the dangerous oratory of Robespierre & a cigarette in the corner of Albert Camus' mouth. I remember how Dostoyevsky contemplated the ideas that might occur to a severed head during the very few moments it was seeing its body departing forever, the distracted glance of its terrified eye & blood flooding the block of the guillotine like a sacrifice for justice & "its long procession of punishments." But I don't know what this guillotine is that has terrified so many people by its name, just as I don't know what it is that is horrifying me.

What I know will always remain little, little & useless.

Whenever I got a ticket I saw myself dead in an accident, and in every piece of meat I chew I'm eating some human being and I don't know who.

My eyes move as if they were reading a continuous warning that is neither seen nor could easily disappear: Do not say this word. Do not ask for forgiveness. Do not prolong any apology.

Then my eyelids close as if it were the final closure of the eyes of a severed head.

I know that the tired are called by the roofs of towers to give their bodies as a gift to the fence spikes

& that highways insist they throw themselves beneath car wheels

& that the cleanliness of pharmacies with their neon hits seduces them to steal what will hypnotise them forever.

But I disappeared from my own memory, or maybe I vanished & remember no-one.

And because of my excessive silence, everything I think of is erasing me: I am everyone with whom I've talked.

In this huge stillness no idea is my own any more, here where I recall no name that hasn't terrified me & don't remember anyone to whom I didn't apologise, I called those I thought of as friends & invited them to an empty house in order to ensure they'd understand this joke I could never tell well & so experience my absence.

Then how beautiful their sighs were & how real & true.

***

The sparrow that flew down from the washing-line recognized me without knowing my name. His legs were thinner than the line, weak but they served his needs well. I terrified him when I appeared & the terror took his wings high & away. He doesn't differentiate between all of us who are called human; it's the same whether it's me or someone else since his shining eyes don't feel safe with any of us. But I hate it that I keep watch over the name I was given to capture me, that I drag it & it drags me, and that it's stuck to my face & has become part of my voice. Sometimes it seems strange to me when I read it or hear it, or it bores me & I detest it. Like everyone I have spent a long time imprisoning myself in my name, since all of us are buried alive, each in his own: a grave of fear & delight & misunderstanding.

RESTLESS HOLIDAYS

(*from* **Children, Madmen And Animals**)

AUSTERLITZ

Yesterday I left for another yesterday
hungry as a drunk guest
lost in the dawn of his own self.

On the way there,
I lie down under the towering chestnut trees
like a child hiding under a bed soon to be covered by clouds.

THE LOCK

Tedium made me forget my fears
so I got used to this house:
remorsefully, I shut my mouth;
alone, I open my heart.
I am my happiness and my dereliction.
I open the book and close it and open it again,
freeing in a small victory
the door of a grave
I pull tight on my self
like a child hiding away in a closet.

A WELL IN A DISTANT CEMETERY

Under a walnut tree planted by a raven
there's a well that a madman dug with a needle
so that ink gushed forth.

The word was.
Swaying inward toward the page
like a lantern descending a white-washed well
its rope in the hand of a child.

THE KABBALA'S PARROT

Like a tongue with wings of water
the island begins to stir.
Go there and descend the stairs to the Alley of Swans
and sigh in front of its playing cards: How lovely!
Go there and disappear laughing, behind the queens & jokers,
behind the good and bad omens dozing like the eyes of a Siamese cat.
Let your voice be proof of such telepathy,
be the Book's tongue,
and let the Kabbala's parrot fly off at dawn to hover over you,
singing you his only song
and leading you, lulled solitary one, through the Library.
Wake up,
a large cloud has risen from the steaming river,
it will wander through the aisles, erasing with its hand the titles & names
on the spines of the books, erasing the works of
sages, historians–al-Tabari, ibn al-Athir–the beginning & the end.
In the silence of this holiday,
a voice is heard–it's you –
mingling a shaft of sunlight–the rare missing one –
with ancient, plentiful ink and dust.
From now on you will find nothing.
You will lie down alone in the cave of words, grounded by amazement,
beside a wooden mouse-trap,
and we–the mice of books–will be the bait with which you catch Time,
before it's killed with us in its belly, saved only for a moment.
No-one will know what happened to us.
We will become the dreams of the girl who fell asleep in front of the tv.
The documentary carries on:
a volcano whose eruption has subsided on an island in the north.
Its ashes cover the sand,

and a lizard with its snout and tail is rolling a raven's egg
across that hot surface to the edge of the ocean
to send it floating off for eternity like a tiny doorless palace
that will be waiting for you this evening amid the snows.
You will not see it.
The raven's egg is bluish white and as speckled as your socks.

BLOOD ON THE STAIRS

What's this grimace when
the cackling stops of a sudden?
The river of words is shallow,
the dead were swimming in it before you.
Stretch your lower lip.
Insert the blade.
Let speech bleed.

PARTY'S END

Be off, I beg you.
Hurry up. Go away.
Leave me & don't worry.
Leave me alone to weep
as if I were my mother
who weeps to soothe herself
but cannot forget, then
sleep will caress me with oblivion
because I am the child of myself.
Come back to me.

THE CHILD'S REGRET

The film ended.
The rescue boats became coffin lids
and only the coffin lids survived,
floating like you cradled by the waves,
and returning to the beach they'd run away from.
Fishermen pulled them out,
weighed down by salt,
and carried the drowned to their distant villages.

With a ray of torpor,
the moon was stitching patches on your breast
with the fur of a cat as envious of you as you of it.

Dew glittered on its whiskers,
you trimmed them while it slept
and singed the remnants with your cheap lighter.
It stared at you in terror,
as if it would pierce your eyes with its claws
or bite your jugular.
It ran away, escaping you.
You glimpsed a fight that dispersed the smoke of burning garbage,
their tails fluffed like comets are.

It used to come back,
mewling, as hungry as you, under this window,
whenever you threw it out
into a dry valley close to the border
or among the tombstones of Mozan's hills.

This time
it lost its way and never returned …

TREE ASH

The cellar's a sty full of angels
and drunken sailors.
Their weeping wets the bread and straw
and the smell climbs many stairs
before vanishing.
Then a sweet fragrance spreads:
fire turning cudgels
back into the spans of a peach tree.

EMPTY NESTS

Fog is the vapour of a word uttered but never heard.
Perplexed women saw a crescent thinner than a spider's thread
torn apart by fishermen.
Their ears were question marks
whose earrings had fallen in the mud–
shiny as the eye of a parrot
which has come to learn just a single word :
Farewell.

UNDER SPRING SKIES

I glimpse the black scissor
of a swallow veering through a high ball of mosquitoes,
but snow is not woken from its cloud slumber
by such slight shrilling
and water does not recall its silver swords.
The dust of lindens has dried
the pollen on the soft down of bees.

What was slowly offered by the shadows on the plain
is smoke that has suffused the edge of my collar:

Spring is an empty black carriage
behind which vehicles slow down
on deserted roads,
and my dark hand–
stretched between my cheek and the setting sun–
is a mirror calling out for the missing child.

CLIFFS

Light is throwing its immense feather
between the church tower and the shop of coffins
where I stood yesterday
and waited for someone to take me to the mountains
and I didn't see the vehicles with their monotonous
pulse that lulled us to sleep for years on end.
Daylight is beckoning my footsteps
like a friend whistling under the window
to climb those distant stairways.

*

The light wind drowned our white papers.
Blue ink bled into the swimming pool
and kohl-coloured evening covered what we'd written
and we opened the top buttons of our shirts,
lightweight sails that make nothing move.
At daybreak, on the remains of a floating poem,
we saw a crimson dragonfly landing
like a sole surviving word.

SNOW

My life brings tears to my eyes
like the generosity of the deprived,
an idiot considering her face in a lift's mirror.
You named my tears errors of interpretation.
You called the world a conflict between me & myself.
You struggled instead of me, and I talked in place of plants
until the sap you pumped up the stems of plastic roses evaporated
and the endings amputated the tongues of beginnings.
I said: my obscenity is the vengeance of my timidity.
I was weaker than the breath of life, and others owned the wings.
You ordered me: you have the right to live.
What you said is significant but impossible to listen to.
You warned me against being alone.
So forgive what I have understood. I will never forget it:
we paint the mud in the cold with our spit and name it snow.
The surface cracks,
so that the fissures will sing of another surface
and when the parrot awakens there
the crime takes place and echoes return: "There is
one scar at least burning sometimes, neither seen nor forgotten.
Let random chance interpret reality
since words neither flourish nor increase their number nor fly."
Consciousness is indeed obscene.
I was alone and therefore I loved you.
You forced me to sit like a half-boiled egg
in the dish of a fevered child,
and you urged me:
"Eat your eyes.
And every night learn how to shut up and to die."
Stroking my hair
You glued the spray of your laughter to my face
like recklessly shot sperm
then you got up of a sudden

and turned your backs on me to read newspapers.
Did I faint that you let me
gather the iron dust of words as if I were a magnet
so as to read in my palms what's killing me
and pay the price of gentle grace?
Did you get bored that you amused yourselves terrifying me
and made me wear this mask, pointing at me with raised
eyebrows: this is our clown?
Did you rape me while I was asleep–
under the semen tree
or on a couch you'd tightly tied me to
like the name of a pliers to the plier?
I don't know. I don't recall. I can't remember. I don't want to.

(Many agreed, and the others are always many, experts and sages who know how to relax and how to shake cities with their male orgasms, when it's said: does a guest have the right to be angry !? Forget it. You're either dreaming or pretending. This is what you wanted. So cheer up and don't invent another lie).

How I stared at the phone
like a slave pleading his deaf trader,
deluded by its semaphore or ringing
as if some message or voice
might assuage or unvoice my speech.
Let them take me to hell.
Let me take myself to hell.
Not to boast but to be healed.

I don't believe what I am saying.
Little by little the world returns to me,
without either secret or truth.
It's raining and I'm thinking of snow.

TONGUE TATTOO

Under a rainbow
which the dead had planted in the mud,
I walk between your two walls,
a corridor closed off by a pile of chairs,
a blind corridor which sleepwalkers pass through in a broken-down train
& they stumbled over al-Mutanabbi who's asleep & reading no-one else
& they became female & melt before us into the sky's red ribbon.
Did you hear the snowflake falling,
between a knee that knows the shame of steps
and a hair that knows the scandal of the head?
The waiting room is the body of a child
in whose ear Satan whispers "you are alive."
Our photographs are being sold as black & white souvenirs
& the rail lines are crosses made from matchsticks & the bones of children.
The wind which came before us stopped above our heads,
frozen like a transparent stone.
To the right, the library is empty in a cave & soldiers are washing their helmets
in the fountain's tears.
To the left, the church is cold as a dragon sleeping under a waterfall.
In front of us, a sun shining like a thunder-bolted head in a tree of steel.
I hear whistling.
I tie a stone to my wrist & walk between your walls.
The smile which fenced in my weakness
quietly collapsed.
The touch which lightly passed across the sleep of things
dried in the palm of my hand.
My life is folded like a used face-rag
in the pocket of a roaming peddler,
with which I would wipe death's nose
when he's done with sobbing on my shoulder.

BUBBLE

The story is an unspeakable pain in another unspeakable story.
Whenever I described something I erased what I feel.
I didn't look with my eyes so I saw none but myself,
I see what I understand so I neither see myself nor anyone else.
Who touched me violated me.
What lulled me made me sleepless.
Wherever I sat I was rooted,
gazing into grief,
so departing seems more difficult than the journey.
The penitence in my eyes isn't enough to light the way back.
Will I survive this survival?
What will happen
if I travelled
and bit on the rope of patience
and begged and ran mad in the country of others?
My left hand is widowed.
Behind me someone's looking at my right hand:
a smashed hand with its fingers intact
crawling in front of the torn lips of those who'd spoken.
Eavesdroppers were many, so slips of my tongue become many, like nonsenses.
Then they overlooked them and rescued me to despise me.
I was asked my opinion and it evaporated like stammerings of guilt,
I blurted things out, as if undressing myself,
I grabbed at air as a drowning man grabs at hair.
I was accused whether I kept silent or spoke,
And my language slowed down and lost balance
like a bubble with its air rotted
and I popped it on the tip of my nose.
I was being chased inside my delusions,
my coinage vanished suddenly like criminals,
my pennilessness was repeated again and again but my fear never vanished:
I was scared by whoever I saw not seeing me,
by what scandalises messages,

by whoever yanked my ear
to keep me alive standing on tiptoe.
They scared and concealed me–
The angry, the horrified, the cynical, and informants on bicycles–
and I was pushed toward my end
by what I forgot and by whom I met,
so I believed what was said,
then I believed what was not said,
and all these ruses tricked me
and the fault remains unforgiveable in me
and nothing happened in my passing life,
my life that never happened.

A LIGHT IN WATER

(partly after Bill Viola)

(Innumerable Attempts To Reach Eternity)

The simple but impossible method of achieving immortality is to stop breathing, then to stay alive without breath.

The dreamers are sleepers fully dressed under the water. Bubbles are a sign of life, as of the body's decay. We can't be sure which. They sleep on the stage and their hands don't move, and the waves delude you into thinking their fingers stir in weak and final motions.

An illuminated column writhes in deep waters, a young man's plunge as a comet swallowed by a whirlpool; we were in front of those waters and he didn't see us standing there, behind us the great conflagration. Bubbles, stars come up from the depths, were merging together, increasing in size as they surfaced towards us. We all are black shadows in this great light, unless the huge fire be damped down. No-one will see us as long as the conflagration is behind us and no-one will see us if we are inside it.

Did we go far or get close or will we melt soon? We heard the sea's roar in the desert, our faces were touched by hot air blowing through the windows of the cars we were crammed into. Immaculate brightness dazzled our eyes. Dry waves ascended like transparent tongues above flames beneath a burning sun. So this is a mirage! I love it neither as symbol nor metaphor but as phenomenon. I delight in being deluded by my eyes.

***

(The Painting)

Among the body-parts, after death, the hand is what most resembles its bones.

You are not a documentary film. You are a painting. No events are happening here so don't expect anything. Inside the painting there is another painting and a faint ray of light passes through that frame to fall on a solitary book whose letters are tiny and as wide open as your lungs. The same ray illuminates the knitting needle inserted by a woman into a skein of wool. A spider's thread shines on a potted cactus; there's no escaping fragility, there must be a breeze for you to see such tenderness in a thin thread that summarizes your destiny.

Very slowly the painting moves from screen to screen. The changes are slight. On the first screen, the woman who disappeared is sleeping naked, that candles might be lit behind your eyes on another screen. Had you slowed down you would have seen all of this. Don't rush things. Don't be the one on whom slowness is forced, don't be the convalescent or the old man. Slow down exactly when you might be hurrying off. Put on your clothes without haste. Do everything in slowness. Perhaps you will find some sort of solution or hope.

The painting is still hanging on the same wall, and if you stretch your hand out towards the woman asleep inside there, you will see a hand slowly opening its fingers underwater.

***

(The Screens)

Between the two screens there's a barrier that's like a threshold between the mirror and the world. On each screen a figure is standing, holding himself together, breath-stopped in front of a dark liquid, then the man in the red singlet begins to cry, and after him the woman in the blue singlet starts crying, too. Are they runners, wanting to reach genuine tiredness after long exertion, the tiredness of the body that silences the tinnitus of death? You will not recognise a man sobbing in his solitariness. First you see the reflection of his face distorted by his tears in the pitch dark of water, then you see how these tears melt his face. No sounds are audible. You are watching the strangled weeping of two people, each the shadow of the other; a man and a woman exchanging roles, entering the black mirror only to leave it the next time round.

Every face is a reversed mask placed on water. The nose and the mouth are open but no-one can breathe easily. Gasped-out, trapped sighs are blown into the water: we can see bubbles but can't hear the bubbling, and the gap between water and air is as narrow as that between life and death, a barrier of two centimetres. We will always see someone crying, standing surrendering themselves before water.

***

(The Jump)

We saw him in the distance, naked. When he came close to us we found that he'd dressed on the way. How that happened when the land is so open we don't know. A man unknown to us, he has remained here, whereas his physical movements were taking place in parallel times. He stood for a long while at the edge of the water without throwing himself in; he remained standing there, lowering his head and closing his eyes. But when he did jump his leap was incomplete. He remained held in mid-air as if transformed into an image of a world suspended above water, whereas ripplings were wrinkling its surface. This water on the earth, inside a square stone frame, is not a mirror but a painting more ancient than ourselves.

At this moment, the man is suspended in mid-air like a diver or a foetus, his body a ball, and nothing is holding him in place; around him small leaves and fruits are dropping from the beaks of birds that are flying above him, though we cannot see them. Maybe a sparrow is feeding its young a large butterfly whose wings are crumbling in its beak and the wing dust settles on the water's face and wrinkles slightly there.

Slow down. Had you looked longer you would see. Above the water it was night with a half moon and just a few stars, but high high up the air still had the light of day. Immeasurable time had passed through this stillness, before a weeping willow covered a man who tried to jump. Was he thinking to swim, or of death? We don't know. We don't know the depth of anything we see. In this quiet rustling, if you come upon thick leaves and branches that touch the water, try to look for the openings: there's someone we don't see, like this man who tried to jump; like a hand stretched out to a drowning man, his shadow trembling over the face of the water, until little by little it vanished entirely. What remained were the soil, the water and the trees.

***

(*The Meanderers*)

They take off their phosphor helmets and coarse gloves, and lean their backs against the rocks in the evening. They've tied the chains back on the cranes, and cut the ropes of the hanged with animal shears, leaving a woman alone, praying at the edge of water, her arms folded and her hair white.

Everyone realized that speech was unnecessary. The rescue crew and construction workers are on stage, their theatre in front of ancient trees beneath a cloudy sky, but the crowd becomes bored and ambles on, thinking that nothing's happening here.

*

We travel to look back. We travel and we look back and we still see the quiet file that has been moving slowly through the forest behind us since dawn. Are those the same people who go back and forth rehearsing the same scene? Are we hypnotized by repetition? It's daytime now and you gently pass your fingers over the forehead of the sleeping woman, kissing her as if consoling someone who is dying, your slow motion all tenderness.

*

You knock a long time on the door of a dying man you left alone a short while ago, lying on his old marriage bed. You are listening for his breath but you hear nothing. You keep listening until it's your own breath you hear and it's death knocking on the door of your heart; and if the door is opened you will not see the waxen face or toothless jaw. Someone has locked the door and thrown the key into the great water, then left. A cab that had been waiting for him in front of the entry stairs took him away.

*

A grandfather clock resembling a large wooden headstone, its two hands still rotating, tolls midday. A river gull perches on its crown. The old man and old woman are sitting on two chairs, close by their things that fill the boat that's sailing away now, their bedroom mirror between them. Their house is sailing off with them inside it, crossing the great water slowly. We, who always watched them from our balconies and windows, are left behind, as if we were the dead.

***

(The Deluge)

You don't notice anything because you see like someone who remembers.

Like a prophet in a film, be the camera.

Meanwhile the entire city passes by: on the sidewalk a homeless man holding a piece of cardboard: I am hungry. The benefactor, the preacher, and the one who pities each approach him, but in the end it's an air hostess who accompanies him beyond your field of vision. A lady carrying an orange tree crowned with just a few oranges passes by, another lady walking cautiously and carrying a large china bowl passes by, and more than once the same man carrying books balanced between his hands and his chin, elderly and bald with round eye glasses. Men with flyers pass by, a lady carrying an empty cat basket, a man carrying a large maquette of a house and behind him a small girl wearing shoes larger than her feet and carrying a bear doll. A lady pushing a pram containing a bonsai pine, a small child whose red balloon bursts in front of him. And a large rolled-up carpet carried by two wall-painters. A young woman descending the stairs and remembering before leaving the building she'd forgotten something, and you understood it was her black bag. Many bags pass in front of you, some people clutch one in each hand. Someone carrying a cheap chandelier, a lady whose shopping-bag bursts and a young man helps her to gather her spilt groceries before quickly leaving. People arguing and shouting without noticing you're there. A tall girl opening her parasol for her less tall mother, a group of women in mini-skirts whose calf muscles are strong, men who look back as if their pockets might have holes, a priest carrying a box with a parrot in a cage tied on top. Someone carrying a column of grey hats and another carrying a television and a third carrying a heavy blanket in a transparent bag. Then you see most of those who have passed before you returning from the opposite direction, doing the same things, each acting as if they were the porter of their own lives. Are those who were in a rush the same ones who escaped with their skins? Has all this scene been taking place in a mirror? What is the difference now between the original and the copy, the image and its reflection, sleep and wakefulness? Don't leave, illusion. What does it matter if the deluge comes.

BOX OF PAIN

I support you, who are weak like me,
not as two hands support the chins of sages,
not as a disabled man holds up another,
not as a cane with which the blind stab
leaves fallen onto narrow pavements
not as a ball on which clowns balance,
as if it were one final last planet
rolling over this mad one.

I'm far away but brace you in your solitude,
as an index finger rises past a widow's cheek,
wobbling like an arrow just as it's being shot,
a salt crystal glimmering on its tip,
returning to the eye that shed it,
submerged in shadows & wings.

*

If the dead were buried,
how would pain be buried?
What is the point of cursing the curse?

Life is loss.
And this silence the heaviest.
How slowly do words
flow & become rusted in the blood of night
or rise up like sap to the dusty leaves.

The branches are brawling & shaking
but there is no wind.

Right now, as lonely as you,
as our mother, as this tree,
another bird has fluttered up that we didn't see.

The house of screaming is jagged out,
a diamond cracking the world's grimy pane.

*

You weren't there at daybreak,
when patients, passengers & soldiers
with bald or shaven heads
loomed like far-off windows from dark huts.
There was a hazy mist which didn't last that long,
the boy crossed it in front of the hospital gate
where he found a pistol in the grass.
You were not there.

Now you're a story being told in a place you're not.
Your throat, that box of pain,
is full of bones & feathers.
In the white of your eye
there's a blood spot, small & rusted,
like a sun setting in the distance
over a snow field
trampled down by straggles of hungry soldiers.

MISTAKE

You lost the bet,
from the very outset you lost it.

The soul was not a bird,
you hatched its egg with your two fangs,
the egg which was being orphaned in the chimney
by the ghost of childhood.

The soul was not
a mottled downy butterfly
to be caught whenever you were bored,

not a leaf to be placed on the wall to dry
so it could be crushed beneath your heel anytime you wanted.

The soul is sad blood which spotted the earth,
sanguinely & voicelessly,
like the threads of a first menstruation.

THE MIRACLE

Yellow trees are rolling their apples
over the shoulders of the pale hills.
The raven is asleep
in the belly of the dead white horse,
spinsters are taking their rest in evening's windows.

This long grass will not hide you:
the pit of your plum killed a bat.
That time will never pass:
I was almost touching you
but you turned and went away
without disappearing.

When does your loneliness end?
How will the dark of the vanished trees disappear?

I will not wake you,
because I've become lonely like you,
like someone looking for a lost ring at a feast;
Clowns have placed a cinder in my mouth
and the miracle made desperate
has devoured the path extending between us.

HEIRS & STROLLERS

The stage is crammed with tables & napkins.
A deep quiet with no-one there.
An important paper went missing,
            expenditures of wars that never happened.
Thieves buried mirror shards in the mouths of the burgled.
Politicians belched onscreen.
Won't anyone utter the dead man's name?
The physician considered a rusted scalpel & complained:
            "The shroud has no pockets!"
He waved at the patients & visitors,
motioning them to go for a stroll.
"Then come back & don't be so suspicious.
Don't leave this courtyard. You'll be in danger."
They wandered inside the walls until they were lost.
In the corridors, employees distressed by flatulence,
            tranquil as yawning cows,
                        chewing on carrots & green beans,
heard him anxiously stutter before he hid away:
"Where are the salt eaters going, gobblers of void & rumour?
I'm run mad. And you… you're bored by Paradise."
Paradise was a contagious word,
            a garden without stars
                        whose boundaries are rooted in sand,
                        whose stones ate away at our shoes,
and we were exchanging flowers
            and countries: ambassadors
                        and morgues: corpses of the unknown.

from A SOLDIER IN A MADHOUSE

"Slow it!" when the raid came
and they gagged men with their leather belts,
my scream turned back in my throat
and wore away what was left of my language.
The numbness in my arm awakens,
too often had I lain upon it,
and I see all those who were staring at me just now
and the sutures of the air are unpicked as if they
            are my mouth and I hear nothing,
I stare at the dot in the dirty white
as it turns out to be an eye staring back at me,
and wherever I looked I found myself multiplying.
There are stares devouring me, they leave nothing but
                                                  a crust,
if I touch it with my fingertips I'd vanish.
I am the bread of the invisible:
how terrified I am by the eyes of the terrified,
everyone who's terrified, terrifies.

AUTUMN HERE IS MAGICAL AND VAST

A bloody shaft of light
shone under our door between their compass & the north star
so the road passed through our house out toward the estuary.
Its stones are our tears which silted in our chests until we spat them out.
The road smashed the Janus-faced mirror & the perfumers' flasks
and left us nothing but the clouds to dwell in,
with our mouths, like our pockets, stuffed with sand.

***

Rains taught him how he'd evaporate from the earth's body.
The cat taught him how to sleep in the shadows of roses.
The well led him to concealment.
The leaves are going yellow, shouting, whirling about,
so he listens to the pulse of the tree.
The world comes tearing through,
tatters fluttering like banners in the amphitheatre
where madmen swam in our wounds, pleading they'd not heal,
nothing will stop all this blood but the sun & the wind.

***

Our dreams remember our dreams.
Like drenched cats we took shelter under the tree when it rained
and large droplets put out our cigarettes.
Flashlights moved across the theatre of clouds.
The hankies were sodden. Chairs were abandoned
where I waited for your hand.
Roots lifted the pavement slabs in front of us
and I concealed your craving on my shoulder
like the tattoo of an unfulfilled desire.

***

The drowned came back with pebbles & the stove was
black as a burnt pot.

The scissors in your hand are the tail of a dead swallow
& your heart is weaving light shafts & straws as one rug.
The moon of your prayer is full,
it will share its body's loaf with you
& roll like a grindstone of chalk over the cloth of evening.
We will wear what the blind wear,
meanwhile the wrinkles pain raises with its hooves inside your guts
crowd into the corners of your mouth & eyes:
no place but your face.

***

There is a sea tossing & perspiring under the soil,
& a young man sobs because he's seen bread. This is your son.
Stretch out your hand & push at this rock with your touch.
From beneath the headstone a thirsting wave comes forth
& places a kiss on the palm of your hand,
quiet as this grass, slight as the scarf on your head.

***

If you came back alive to your mother
you would see her tattoos drop blue as perfume,
you would see her mouth's
blood-red cracks,
the names peeling from her salty lips,
you would hear her tongue which made god descend
to smell insomnia's remnants in the rooms' corners.

You would come back
hungered as an idea you're afraid would die,
and if you opened any door,
to reassure yourself or to leave,
you would open perplexity.
The mirror would come closer, higher.
Like two old enemies
your eyes gaze into your eyes.

MR. NOBODY LISTENING TO HIS OWN STORY AT THE COURT OF KING ALCINOUS

White olive flowers, poking from scorched trunks,
 I smell them in the moonlight.
It's mid-May. I hear the tender slap of your hand against its lower branches,
that glimmer in the orchard night, their silver leaves rippled
 by the breeze across their sheen of dust,
An owl flutters up–your son nurtured it like a tiny grouse in a guest-room,
 it lives camouflaged like you, the door of its cage open, its eyes yellow
 as narcissus eyes,
it will fly off tomorrow, in the dead of day, to tell your life to the vast prairies,
 your life I fashioned from my own.
Will death then be so slightly drawn back
 that God will cast his shadow across my blind eyes,
 and shade my days that run between his hands,
 a rosary beaded by a prisoner from tiny fruit pits?
When would the sea reach my bed without breaking over me,
 a wall silvered by the sweat of our souls?
The moon–above the hills–is a silver bell.
The dew on the grass is the urine of the terrified who couldn't escape.
The darkness dilates its coal-black eyes
 (one of them a god's dead from terror, the other a drowned son's)
and time lain down between them, a bullet
 shot by mercy into the forehead of terror.
I will hear in my final moments,
 a prayer in a language I don't understand,
and I will be happy.

*

Ships laden with cargoes of glances cast their anchors on the sea-floor of my head,
above them a sky that is not this sky
 and someone waiting on the tiniest of islands for a glance of compassion,

and the one waiting is the double I live with everywhere but can't see,
my insomnia-gossip telling me:

"You're barred, so don't leave.
You're suspect wherever you go.
Soon, the cart of your memory will plunge into another mud
from which you will build another house and say:
'I wish I were there in the dog days of August,
Lying beneath clusters of black grapes muslined by my brothers' old socks,
around which wasps swarm like drunkards.'"

*

With its mouth, Death feeds us black grapes in August,
its tiny eggs stuck to our eyelashes.
Our enemies revived our Gods,
resurrected from the ashes of our homes & the vapour of our blood.
Our friends, with their palms come down on our shoulders
to console us, buried our wings.
No bird of mercy touched our lips with its solitary wing.
No love abrupted our merciless timepieces with its water.
Warm in the lungs are our unsaid words.
And we who are warm because tainted time sleeps under our skin,
heavy because the time that died had crammed our tongues & bodies
with smashed stones that are no-one's home any more.

*

We are burdened with what we avoided,
we are burdened by what we haven't done.
We befriended here those we ran away from there.
Our light casts no shadow. Our bodies leave no trace.
A black ray of light had arrived before us,
with it the tailor of the world sewed the rend between

earth & heaven,
so another night poured over us,
this long, white night,
and freedom descended stairs we hadn't seen,
burying itself in our midst, beneath grass & stones.
The ray is as black as our eyes,
we see its traces wherever we look,
shining in the corners of funeral notices & threadbare cloaks,
and with it a doll tied back the hair of its sleeping child,
and with it I throttled the voice inside my head,
tied my shoelaces & came to listen to you saying:
We heard our story being told before us,
& we kept silent, loathing our weakness,
& we withheld the tears we had saved for our sins.
They told us metaphors that we found laughable,
we heard that a wound is a window & a mirror,
in which a white hand waves
while we pause to rest in its shade, but photographers hunt us
down like snipers,
a white hand that tied my heart to a snake's tail
and hung from your ears earrings that glinted like tiny hailstones.
They made us hear: "Your pain is lighter when narrated by others.
Your name is your stigma, your name is your heaven,
so dig a grave in your name & illuminate it with pain,
and stay as you are, in your wandering,
detained in this city or that,
a book no-one can understand,
a heavy book that will be drowned in the flood,
its covers eaten away,
and your name will be obliterated by time
and your black words melted in the black deep.
Say goodbye. Say I am the flower grown from your dirt,
fresh and trembling in the sun.
I am the lie you believed in & that I believed to escape you,
and if you uproot me, all the metaphors will shatter."

*

Grand ideas leapt from the mountain tops and plummeted
to our lowest depths:
our good luck, that they'd failed in their attempts to fly.
The droplet that came back from hell without being evaporated,
that drop had fallen from the thirsty man's lip
and sank into the sand to the depths of no meaning.
So be patient with me & don't reproach me for being late.

That year will never pass,
it will poison at every moment every beat of the heart:
They all stared at you in silence,
knowing you would reach a cul-de-sac on the river bank.
So wake at daybreak and don't insist I come at once.
I will fold away the old letter that yesterday embraced your face.
Cover with your palm the sparrow's heart held in your chest.
Follow an ant as it climbs the stalk of a rose.
I am Death & I have no stories for you.
I am your redeemer & your healer,
and if you bleed once again, don't ask for help:
this is your blood, even if drunk by the sun,
this is your harvest, even if of ashes.

*

The world is worse than it was this morning, sadder, quieter.
The far-off figures were still small when they arrived
like this drizzle.
They drowned in our pores, they clutched at our eyelashes,
they floated on the water of our dead feelings.
I lay down, whipped even by the rain, cast naked onto shores,
one shore after another.
So, have I arrived?

Everything pales on arrival,
restraining me, I the disguised one, surrounded by those who'd had hope
& those who were angry.
I would have narrated another story, had I escaped.
Words are abundant before any arrival & after every departure,
they bounce off everything like heavy rain, until they resemble dust.
No stories are left to tell their story.
I haven't become a murderer, even if my hands frightened me,
and bewilderment scared me often in the night.
I had not realised which terror was the most extreme.
I foreswore my responsibility & blamed it on the ruins,
I hid from those who cursed me because I'd left stealthily like a thief running
away from killers,
and I attributed to myself stories that hadn't happened to me.
I lied to those who sheltered me, I managed not to stutter, and said like a man castigating
a child:
"I'm not a stranger, so what am I guilty of? When is the punishment due ?"
I don't know. I don't know this ceiling: my breath, don't abandon me as I sleep.
Where I had plunged into myself–a child crawling at his mother's funeral,
an old man sleeping through the clamour of a wedding–
dreaming of what I can never remember, there in the distance where nothing is
more distant,
nobody can distinguish the drowned from the saved.
Nobody can distinguish the drowned from those swimming.

*

The sky that had dried up the sea crumbled into it,
the fallen gods & the rocks of a rainbow
buried their cradles of waves
like a building collapsed over sleeping children.
A black ray of light coloured the faces of the drowned.
A solitary gull soars slowly at no great height,
lost like light in a desert of blue dust.

*

Whenever a god retreats or sleeps
        he's killed by his worshippers.
I knew nobody closely, because all were disguised as beggars:
        cunning gods, penniless lovers, fathers humbled by their dark skin,
                outrageous sons.
The sky wore a mask, the clouds dragged their heavy skirts,
        the sunset blazed a tremendous masquerade.
It didn't rain. The wind shook old drops off the sycamore branches.
The full moon shone like a trick to blind us.
The weight we lost during the wars
        enabled us to fit our old clothes again.
We went back to what we'd piled up as alms & forgotten in bundles & closets:
        socks we'd stuffed full of marbles & chalk for playground games,
        tattered gloves,
        shoes more wrinkled than our foreheads,
        baggy trousers we'd dress scarecrows in if we managed to cross the border.
I coloured my rags and became a beggar, baffled at my courage,
a poor man playing the role of another poor man, falsifying my papers,
        collecting my debts from those who hadn't killed me.
I carried my moonlit night in the night of all souls
        and trotted like a mouse inside an endless wall,
and I didn't wake the water in which stars were sleeping.
And when I returned to where I was born,
        I who was used to going back had to relive it all over again,
I sought out my companions & dusted from my lips an eternity of speechlessness,
        just as my old swimming dog would shake off all the mud, my dog
                who died on seeing me after all those years,
and I recited to myself the testament our enemies' gods had sent to our gods,
        waiting for a tomorrow where my son waits to bury me.

*

Grief,
in the boat of this breeze you are alone.
Grief,
time preys on life.
Here it is again, a loveless morning a sunless shadow,
then the same short December noon,
and in our hands the knot of insanity that hurt our teeth & bled our fingers
when we tried to untie it.
The child walks through much mud on his way home.
Nobody is in, except for his mother who doesn't hear the door closing.
She doesn't hear because she's singing, and the ginger cat's mewing on the threshold.
She's singing in her loneliness
and steam from the soup runs down the window pane in the kitchen,
on the far side of the immense courtyard
where ants eat the lice in the lining of coats
and butterflies collect their debts in years of drought
and big teardrops shed by a sleeping girl dry under the apple tree …
When the son comes closer, his mother thinks it's the wind
so she calls out: "Come in, come in, take sweet tea with lemon.
The door is open, all of us are guests, like you.
Ah, my words, smoke of the fire in my liver."
You who took your first steps at your mother's funeral,
now carry in your arms the child you once had been, light & transparent.
You are still that same child.
Nothing changed. Nothing.

*

Our names become homeless.
Who forgets forgives who remembers.
Who took refuge in departure wishes to take leave of life.
We filled small rooms with the whispers of the humiliated,
we filled trains with our sacks,
green buses with our badly-bandaged wounded,

bulldozers with our memories, boats with the weight of our silence, the world
with our fears.
Then we sat amid the crowd where nobody usually sits,
the traffic lights gave out, the post boxes were smashed.
We lay down in a small park reached after a long walk, and we prayed to be in fear
of nobody,

We didn't play with our phones so as not to terrify the neighbours,
that they not mistake our laughter for thunder
or backfiring motorbikes or the firecrackers of teenagers come in
from the suburbs.
We have with us a city that has departed the present,
and a child who feeds a famished animal that has gone to a corner to die.
We can't know when what is no longer intact will collapse.

*

Earth will smoke us.
Your soul will rise up like a house built on the smoke of a cigarette,
and will ponder in its ascension your body
like a streetlamp gazing at ruins on a crowded street.
Earth smoked us.
And we were on the surface of her mirror while she bathed in the milk of the
galaxies,
and we trod with care over the misty surface until we reached a conflagration
in another zone,
where we slipped enough to break our necks on the spilt water of those who had come
to extinguish it
and then prayed "may the end be the beginning."
We kept on walking, immersed in the earth's breath.
And we opened a huge door in the fog, not knowing where we were entering.
And we found ourselves in front of the bad omen of a square ultra-white façade.
With errant glances we went through its revolving doors, black as our eyes.
We only muffled our sighs when no more security bars remained in front of us
and no crimson alarms rang out

to expose the knives hidden in our silences.
We could smell in photographs the stench of dandies and heavily made-up women,
and beheld jostling crowds with a thousand fears shining in the pores of our skin.
Had we entered a furnace since those who cursed us cried out: "Is that hay or dry dung
inside your heads?"
Or had we kept walking, no longer knowing whether we were smoking or dying of cold,
going forwards or backwards, with the future closing its circle around us
like a lost ring & we its severed finger?
We opened the door and our breaths entered before us and so did the fog: immense
as the question we'd brought with us through the valleys & fields & hospital corridors,
and quick as the darkness, quicker than our hesitations,
coming from alleyways where patients sit on thresholds
sleepless as we are at daybreak, their foreheads wrapped,
drinking light-coloured tea,
cursing the wounds that hurt when they laugh.
In this white blindness I stretched my hand out towards what I could not see
fingering words that were crushed like snails underfoot on a road not taken,
under the sun that disappeared after burning our eyes
to show us the darkness it conceals.
Some words stopped growing and turned back to console us like silent dogs,
but the fearful are blind and deaf.
We had gone so far inside the die, suspended in its immense darkness.
Who is the enemy this time? Whose hand is the thrower?
Onto which shore will we be cast?

*

The roar bursts my closed ears.
I wish I had never had any fear.
I want the least of it, this world too much for me.
My pleasure is to remember in silence, my body thinning to air.
I forgot the names of streets & meals, I forgot the songs.
I forgot what I read, where I walked, what I'd seen and smelled,
where I slept and with whom, how long I remained lying down.

I say to myself, now as all things are muddied together:
"The quiet waters will show us marvels."
Little by little this grey rain will remove the kohl of evening,
and before the train enters the tunnel,
the Suspension Bridge will have been left far behind, and the bougainvillea
crazily climbing the windows,
the umbrella with its ribs broken by the wind
like a spider whose prey had snapped its legs.
In the dimmed glass I will see my face when darkness gives it back to me,
pale and astonished, hungry after a long journey.
Who will I call out to in this intolerable crowd?
How will I become my own self's city?
Wherever my eyes wander I see murderers.
I have to look for my own murdered.
I will start in the mirror.

*

The eye is a slave of what it sees.
Your fear blinded you,
my blindness set me free.

THE SLEEPING FAMILY

With a key hung from her waist our mother opened a door behind which death was waiting for her.

Before this silence, we heard a *ney* playing in the earthen rooms; you heard it before us and told us: all women are *neys*, and all men too, and death—that blind musician—blows through their holes with a mouth of light and a mouth of wind.

We have nothing but this silence–with its forgiveness and its cruelties. With its beak a crow dug out the first orifice between human buttocks and the first cave between the thighs, and the first navel, the first mouth and first two ears, and then it led Cain to the idea of the grave. To kill the idea of the crow, we killed the crow—trainer of us all in the rites of burial, our teacher in the arts of secrecy and theft, prompter of our always turning back like thieves to whatever shines–and the first to be buried by us in all our long wanderings.

My brother plays on a *ney* that I hate and lightning flickers like blood down the veins and alleyways. Music is the night of misfortune and the day of poverty during which our bones are eaten away. Songs float down from blue Taurus to the clay terraces and the *neys* of my brother wander through the nights, light as my mother's bones where the winds whistle.

How much music has shed us. How much we've borne these melancholies. How long we've listened to griefs that weighed down on our chests. This music is ancient because it is our life; with sadness it woke our mother out of the nothingness of blind death. A *ney* that she loved brought her back–a quiet, young girl in this noon-time, tossing behind her shoulders two thin braids–and we are out in the bright light of the uplands, in front of this cave that sheltered us, shading our eyes with our palms and laughing off the torrent of our fears. We will smell on her dress little violets which have mottled a scorched land. And perhaps a flower that we cannot see will give us back our minds, that we will not stuff with words every emptiness that terrifies us.

Our mother is our child. Our mother is younger than our sister and summer is a wedding. Married to the summit of the mountain like snows touched by the hand of morning, carried in the air like a feather or a light scarf, her shadow is blotted out by apricot blossoms that never fade (the roots of the apricot tree buried the foundations of our vanished house); the blossom in the house of our memory will never wilt: on each petal watered by our mother there's a tiny droplet shimmering, a dawn star pulsing in the dead of day.

My brother, on the lip of the well there is a *ney* with which the earth is narrating our days to the stones, and it allows me to hear your silence. The dead are returning to live among us and in one short tomorrow they will accompany us to the clouds, like our mother's tears brushed away by the fingers of a breeze.

THE END OF DAYS

(after Anselm Kiefer & for Elena Lydia Scipioni)

A snake with honey-coloured eyes survived and told what had happened:

In our burning fields, Yesterday drew me with the spittle of its mouth upon a charred wall, like a blackboard in front of frightened pupils. Thus you saw in me the image of my father, throwing my last pennies into the fountain of death, then sewing the buttons of his oil-green coat in the furrows of mud where you had planted seeds, arranged in the form of words, and they grew and blossomed when light rained down, warm as remorse, and again blood was made to flow on the palms of the earth. Canes grew high as poplars and we broke them to roof our refuge, and we jumped over our vein-streams to swim in our first sky. We fertilised our language with our debris. Mountains had become ripe heads for the fists of the sky & the slopes cheeks we ran down like melted ice, and at every point where the disappeared had fallen an unattainable flower sprang up, or a burning matchstick flickered before a schoolboy could close his mouth over it to put out the flame– as he hurries to do his homework on forgetting fear.

We will remember for a long time how we were before this harvest. Each of us will visit his own grave, carrying a whip on his shoulder, or behind his back a sickle or a knife. Time was a game. We bade farewell to our beds that had been smashed by our dreams. Gamblers offered us a moon that crumbled to dust at the touch of our fingers. Rats offered us their eyes as stars. Hunger blazed its suns behind our foreheads. Books we hadn't read flittered down and landed on our ulcers. Great silences seeped through our bandages. No one uttered a word. The dots and signs with which we ended our lines leapt towards the words scattered about them, and all meanings changed.

THE OLD CHRIST

(after Pierre Bonnard & for Jinane Abbadi)

1

There's no cure for this hesitancy.
An unease you're familiar with,
        like a river rippling between two enemies,
                quietly ebbing back.
Who shot you?
The flashbulb befuddled you into losing your balance
        & you duped your fear by smelling a rose
                no one sees in the dust but you,
you the emaciated, who fasted for forty days.
Detesting the touch of water and miracles,
        you created a wedding fish from white wine,
                bathing women from the dust of peaches.
Fascinated by imperfection, you missed the final touch.

2

Who fought you?
Are your fists a little clenched
        because there are camera lenses in every corner,
                and the perplexed & miserable have nowhere to hide?
This evening, God sparks April's lightning,
        photographing what's unseen in the womb.
The dead are blowing a forgotten organ tune in the birch trunks,
and you are standing alone, eyes lowered & chest naked,
        your reddened face a bolted door hammered by hands,
                blistered by the sun & the shame.
        Your tongue abstains from any blow,
you standing alone, a boxer no longer holding brush or gloves
        in an arena he never leaves
        because he is unable to depart,
                not knowing where he can go.

WERE IT NOT FOR THE THREE PLEASURES AFFORDED TO YOUTH ...

The idea that Salvation is catalysed by malady.

No mirror to view my face or nullify my pallor or the asphyxiation of my features. I'll stop worrying. Let me be visited by a punishment I don't deserve. Trembling and helpless, I surrender to the fever.

And I calm down and tell myself:

Deceive life and live as a convalescent, an insomniac, a drunkard:

You, young man I don't know, measure with your lips the temperature of my forehead, before the eye wilts & the glance is broken, before the throat dries up & sweat oozes with scandalous sourness. Craving a heart that cannot be heard, a lucidity that comes after secret grieving, a calm you've never tasted—be someone in a fever who is healed by himself, not a hostage who silently anticipates his execution because the most terrible thing had already happened & he has come to terms with the sentence of death. Be a drunkard whose knees & teeth are shaking from the cold of March. Be someone who sleeps a little, then is knocked over by a blade of grass.

Note: the title is a half line from the Mu'allaqa ('Suspended Ode') of Tarafa Ibn al-'Abd

A NEW LIFE?

A month of cloud came to an end this morning
with a ray of sun entering my empty post-box
with its dust particles, I glimpsed it
as I went out.
Coming back from the night,
with messages of grass from the prisoners' cemetery,
with wet eyes, I talked to myself like a madman,
I switched off my lamp & prepared myself
to begin in silence my day that was splintered by the years
and to step aside slowly on the iron bridge,
amid those running to catch their trains,
a guilty man whose only defence is light.

THE FEATHER AND THE MIRROR

*(A Fairytale from '**God's Cinema**')*

When the Kurd met the she-djinn he was blinded by light and fainted. She put a little mirror under his nose and its silver surface became clouded, then she put a feather there & its down trembled. She felt relieved knowing that he was only asleep and the groanings she heard were not those of death but of his long dreamings: "I love him and he'll stay alive," she said.

The only condition the king of the djinns set on his approval of the marriage of the Kurd and the she-djinn was that he never show anger to her face. The wedding took place in the wilderness for many days and nights, the djinn ignited their eyes like torches out in the mountains that guests might find the celebrations and fires walked in the air among the dancers without burning anyone, and jugs of juice were circulated from mouth to mouth. In order that the djinns not fear any trick from the Kurdish relatives, blacksmiths melted silver pins brought from pillows and dresses and birth gowns, and fashioned necklaces and wristlets with small hammers to give as dowry to the bride.

Days dragged by, months, years. The Kurd and the she-djinn begot children whose skin was white as milk spilt over snow, their fingers tender and pudgy like the cigarettes of mountain folk. And the best-beloved of the Kurd's heart was the stubbornest. One day this stubborn boy disappeared into the wilderness and didn't come back. By the middle of the following day the father returned exhausted from echoing shouts throughout the valleys and caves, and he was enraged by his wife's words: "Don't worry, he'll stay alive and he'll come back." And he forgot his promise and became angry at her. With every word of blame and reproach, a part of her body disappeared and the angry man became blind, seeing nothing. By the time he'd calmed down the wife was entirely gone, and what remained of the children were just half-bodies, but their shadows on the ground were whole. Their mother stayed with them without anyone being able to see her.

WHILE LEAVING A SUNNY ROOM A VOICE CALLED SAYING: "STAY"

The spider's house
in the right angle of the northern window
has not been touched by the wind–
a black house imprinted on your window like traces
of a seal on the stamp of a letter
returned unopened to the sender–
you noticed it when you cleansed your eyeglasses of fingerprints & the dust of days
with a piece of your grandmother's headscarf,
and pulled back a curtain of branches and leaves:
your narrow road still is muddy.

You don't savour the cold.
Were it not for these days, you said,
my life that's been confused by spring
would be a cloud that rained only on me
and changed the colours of that hill from
pistachio-green fluttering above my grandfather's grave
to the sky-blue of my daughter's eyes.

A TREE WHOSE NAME I DON'T KNOW

No bell rings & no-one comes.
How many days have passed
without message or phone call
where I locked myself in & lost the key.
And I too sent no message & phoned no-one.
I who am tormented, bandaged & wilted by words,
I talk to you, tree whose name I don't know:
neither my hunger nor my thirst matter
since I've sucked on the tenderness of your silence.

Alone, I've come to you, to sit beneath your vast mercy;
I am small: a blossom begets me in white oblivion,
a blossom shrouds me, the breeze follows my funeral;
I don't caress girls nor do they caress me,
and like you I don't know my name.
Poor are my words–
that rise & fall like the hiccups of a babe-in-arms–
in the haze of another language,
and my skin talks to you:
with a thousand small mouths it drinks sunlight with you–
the sun of my ancestors whose hair turned white
in their childhoods when they panicked,
terrified by the revenge of wounded serpents;
nobody knew how long the horror would last
or until when the serpents would keep swimming in the waters of dream
until the harsh became tender and the hair at their temples
whitened.

My grandfather aged in his youth;
paralysed by a stray bullet, treatable only by pain:
they laid him down on a rug of goat's hair,
motionless & naked,
they locked the door & windows to his clay chamber

& released the wasps;
in his house, white beneath the April sun,
he waited for quickening pace to return to his feet.

Like him, like you, my waiting has been for too long–
dead hours are my most fertile:
are they happy, the old people of this country I came to
as a guest?
Happiness here is as white as old age;
I see the fearful–infuriated & shouting–
and behind my dark eyes
two gods are slaying a sleeping prisoner.
O, tree whose name I don't know:
each trembling blossom is hope arrived,
your petals have fallen on the crown of my white hair,
and for this long waiting my roots have turned white
like my mother's hair in the dark years;
silently I talk to you–
I whose fear has become sadness
and you who beauty startled into blossom.

CRESCENT

You thinned your pain.

As a boy, on the frontier, you placed it like a small coin under the wheels of a train
        and a girl you loved made herself a necklace from it in the fields.

Smugglers taught you how to strike it in the quiet
        of the night with the hammers of thieves
                to conceal your finger marks in front of others.

You thinned it with silence, with long walks,
        until it became transparent and hard,
                like a cut nail disappeared into the carpet of time.

And when you found it,
        it had become a moon eaten away by love,
                and you hung it in the sky of your soul.

And stayed awake all alone, waiting for the *azhan* of Eid.

THE MUD MILK BAR

(for Jano & Nuh)

After two long days of fear in the streets of our city, this morning, on the phone, my sister let me hear sparrows quarreling over dry bread in the little courtyard of the house they'd moved to several years ago.

An owl soared inside my head, an owl the moon had silvered and sent to us,
descending from the hilltop–where the Yezidis bury each other–
  to the beds installed in front of the houses & on the kitchen rooves,
  fenced in by curtains white as the screens
  where the moon projects its silent films in blue & silver,
  thin-walled boxes with lids removed which sleep has opened
          to the universe;

With the headlamps of his van the driver woke the old man who had been sleeping, ill under the stars of September, so he rose up to receive us, lame, his femur fixed with screws, superstitiously cursing the one who'd invented the name "Death's Fracture," and he slaughtered a rooster for our banquet; his son brought us a home-made arak distilled three times from black figs, a little of which we sprinkled onto plates of tomato & white cheese with black cumin seed, in a tiny shop made of mud. "Lion's milk is heavy on empty bellies," he said & took us outside to sit on straw chairs, where we carried on in silence under God's lamp & iced white arak soothed our palms: a cool breeze brushed our bare arms, coming from the cotton fields, irrigated and blossoming, there where the moon had sent us an owl that swooped down, low and silently, nearby.

Night was spread across wide expanses,
Entrancing was the beating of wings,
Pure, the chanting of insects.

We wandered drunk in the night of our innocence, in the night journey of our return, across the earthen paths that led each of us to the house that was his true home; one among us, who mocked poetry & cotton festivals, who devoured lettuce in secret, fell to his knees, shouting and rolling on the straw ash in his uncle's fields, weeping his lost love, our shirts were muddied by his tears when we carried him, avoiding the last gunshots of those returning from the last wedding of the season, hearing laughter guffawing from loudspeakers as guests burnt garlands of green banknotes. As stealthily as possible we took narrow dark alleys until we reached his home; we woke at daybreak, under the smiles of our sisters: how could we tell the long hard pillows of our mothers from the white watermelons on which we'd lain our heads, like dwarves who place their heads on the fingers of a giant, or like small boys whose palms touch a woman's thigh, while we had been collapsing with happiness, snoring under rustling pine trees on the cold, smooth cement that was hennaed with spots printed by chimneys that had rusted through the winters.

Truth sharpens its fangs on the bones of the forgotten.
Naked is my grown soul.
Owl, you mouth of time that has silvered my temples
                    and savaged the sparrows sleeping on the mulberry branches,
how did you catch the snake whose head my mother tried to trample
                    barefoot in her childhood,
          when it escaped such human fear & lived its long life?
Is it because it closed its eyes like a woman preparing for love,
          and slowed its pace to shed its past?
          Quietly, it took off its leather dress,
          Glimmering under God's lamp amid the blossoming cotton.

A Midsummer Night's Press was founded by Lawrence Schimel in New Haven, CT in 1991. Using a letterpress, it published broadsides of poems by Nancy Willard, Joe Haldeman, and Jane Yolen, among others, in signed, limited editions of 126 copies, numbered 1-100 and lettered A-Z. It now publishes primarily under the imprints:

Fabula Rasa: devoted to works inspired by mythology, folklore, and fairy tales. Titles from this imprint include *Fairy Tales for Writers* by Lawrence Schimel, *Fortune's Lover: A Book of Tarot Poems* by Rachel Pollack, *Fairy Tales in Electri-city* by Francesca Lia Block, *The Last Selchie Child* by Jane Yolen, *What If What's Imagined Were All True* by Roz Kaveney, and *Lilith's Demons* by Julie R. Enszer.

Body Language: devoted to texts exploring questions of gender and sexual identity. Titles from this imprint include *This is What Happened in Our Other Life* by Achy Obejas; *Banalities* by Brane Mozetic, translated from the Slovene by Elizabeta Zargi with Timothy Liu; *Handmade Love* by Julie R. Enszer; *Mute* by Raymond Luczak; *Milk and Honey: A Celebration of Jewish Lesbian Poetry* edited by Julie R. Enszer; *Dialectic of the Flesh* by Roz Kaveney; *Fortunate Light* by David Bergman; *Deleted Names* by Lawrence Schimel, *This Life Now* by Michael Broder; *When I Was Straight* by Julie Marie Wade; and *Our Lady of the Crossword* by Rigoberto González.

Periscope: devoted to works of poetry in translation by women writers. The first titles are: *One is None* by Kätlin Kaldmaa (translated from Estonian by Miriam McIlfatrick), *Anything Could Happen* by Jana Putrle (translated from Slovenian by Barbara Jursa), *Dissection* by Care Santos (translated from Spanish by Lawrence Schimel), and *Caravan Lullabies* by Ilze Butkute (translated from Lithuanian by Rimas Uzgiris).